Bio
Pin
e

Lee, Susan and John
Eliza Pinckney

Weekly Reader Books presents

Heroes of the Revolution

Eliza Pinckney

By Susan & John Lee

Illustrated by Andy Aldridge

 CHILDRENS PRESS, CHICAGO

This book is a presentation of Weekly Reader Books.
Weekly Reader Books offers book clubs for children from
preschool to young adulthood.

For further information write to:
Weekly Reader Books
1250 Fairwood Ave.
Columbus, Ohio 43216

Library of Congress Cataloging in Publication Data

Lee, Susan
  Eliza Pinckney.

  (Heroes of the Revolution)
  SUMMARY: A biography of the industrious young woman
who helped introduce the cultivation of the indigo plant
in South Carolina.
    1. Pinckney, Eliza Lucas, 1723-1793—Juvenile literature.
2. South Carolina—Biography—Juvenile literature.
3. Plantation life—South Carolina—Juvenile literature.
[1. Pinckney, Eliza Lucas, 1723-1793.
2. South Carolina—Biography. 3. Plantation life]
I. Lee, John, joint author. II. Aldridge, Andy.
III. Title.
F272.P642L43   975.7′02′0924 [B]   [92]   76-46445
ISBN 0-516-04658-6

The southern lady is a well-known type. You may have read about her in storybooks. In these stories she was pictured as shy, sweet, and unselfish. Dressed in fine clothes, she sat on her front porch sipping lemonade all day. She was much too helpless for hard work. When there was trouble, she fainted.

The truth is much different. Southern women of colonial times worked at many jobs. They kept gardens, fed hogs, and milked cows. They cooked and they baked. They made lard, candles, and soap. They did their own spinning, weaving, and sewing. They worked from dawn to dusk.

Eliza Lucas Pinckney did all these jobs and more. She taught herself a lot about planting. She studied the soil and the weather. She was not afraid to try new crops. She brought a new plant called indigo to her colony. Because of Eliza, indigo became an important crop in South Carolina.

Eliza came to South Carolina when she was 15. Her father, George Lucas, was an officer in the English army. In 1738, he brought his wife and daughters to the southern colony.

In those days, there was no United States of America. The people lived in English colonies, not states. South Carolina was one of 13 colonies along the Atlantic Coast. These colonies belonged to England. They were ruled by the King of England.

The Lucas family settled on Wappoo plantation. They were six miles up the Ashley River from Charles Town. A creek on the plantation flowed into the river. Twenty slaves worked the 600 acres of Wappoo. They grew crops of rice, cotton, and corn. Colonel Lucas also owned two other plantations nearby.

A plantation was different from a farm. Farms were small. Farmers grew enough food for themselves. They did most of the hard work themselves. Sometimes they had one or two slaves to help. Farmers could make a living, but they weren't rich.

A family with hundreds of acres of land had a plantation. The owner was called a planter. It took many people to run a plantation. Planters bought slaves to do the hard work in the fields. A slave had to do whatever his master ordered him to do. The slave got a place to live, old clothes, and food to eat. The planter got all the money from his slave's work.

George Lucas began to teach Eliza
how to run a plantation. She liked
learning how to make things grow.

"I was very early fond of the
vegetable world," Eliza wrote. "My
father was pleased with it and
encouraged it."

In 1739, Colonel Lucas had to return to army duty. Mrs. Lucas was in poor health. Eliza's father needed someone to take over for him. He left young Eliza in charge of the three plantations.

It was not easy for Eliza to run these plantations. She got up at five o'clock in the morning. Before breakfast she read. Then she walked in the fields to make sure all was going well. After breakfast, she spent an hour on her music. Then she studied French, law, or shorthand. Next, she taught reading to her sister Polly and to several slave children.

During the afternoon, Eliza practiced the harpsichord again. She did needlework and wrote letters. She ordered goods from London. She wrote her two brothers, who were going to school in England. And, of course, she wrote her father, asking his advice on plantation matters.

Eliza enjoyed plantation life. She made wine from grapes. She pickled pork. She sent peach trees grown at Wappoo to a cousin in Boston. During the winter months, she wove shrimp nets and made lace by hand. She shipped eggs to her father in the West Indies.

". . .I hardly allow myself time to eat or sleep . . . ," Eliza wrote.

Eliza took a strong interest in trying to grow new plants. She started a large grove of oak trees. Someday, she hoped to use their timber for ships. She planted a fig orchard. Figs and other fruits made tasty dried sweetmeats.

"The ginger turns out but poorly," she wrote her father one year. Sometimes bad weather killed crops. Sometimes Eliza had better luck when she planted crops in different soil.

In 1739, Eliza's father sent her some indigo seeds from the West Indies. Eliza wanted to try growing indigo plants in South Carolina.

A blue dye could be made from the leaves of the indigo plant. This dye was needed in England. English clothmakers used indigo to dye their cloth blue. They had to buy this dye from the French. The French charged a high price for the dye because it was very scarce. If the colonists could grow indigo, they would sell it to England at lower prices.

Many years earlier, some colonists had tried to grow indigo near Charles Town. They had given up. Eliza wanted to try again. If indigo could be grown, it would become a money-making crop. People in South Carolina needed more money-making crops.

Eliza had to learn about indigo by trial and error. At first she planted the seed at the wrong time of year. She wrote her father. ". . . we had a fine Crop of Indigo Seed upon the ground, . . . the frost took it before it was dry. I picked out the best of it and had it planted, but there is not more than a hundred bushes of it come up . . . . I am sorry we lost this season."

Eliza made other mistakes. She was not sure when to harvest the plant. Once she waited too long. In 1742, she wrote to her father, ". . . the Indigo stood till many of the leaves dropped."

That same year, the seeds he sent
did not come up. The young planter
wrote in her letter-book, "The last
Indigo seed sent was not good. None
of it came up. We shall save enough of
our own to make a Crop next year."

Colonel Lucas tried to help his
daughter. He sent a French dye-
maker from the West Indies to lend a
hand. The Frenchman knew how to
turn the leaves of indigo into dye.

The man, named Cromwell, made
a mess of the job. He told Eliza the
weather was to blame. The truth was
that he ruined the dye on purpose. He
did not want the English to make
blue dye. He wanted the French to
keep control of the indigo business.

"He made a great mystery of the
process," said Eliza. He ". . . said he
repented coming as he should ruin his
own Country by it. . .(He) threw in
so large a quantity of Lime water as to
spoil the colour."

Eliza did not give up. She fired
Cromwell. A black man from the
West Indies took Cromwell's place.
The black man helped Eliza make
the dye. It was not easy to do.

Eliza learned to cut the indigo
leaves at the right time. Then she
soaked the leaves in brick vats full of

water. It took several days for the water to turn the right shade of blue.

When the water turned blue, it was put into other vats. Lime water was added. Then the mixture was beaten with paddles. When it was thick, it was moved to a third set of vats.

In these vats, the dye and water separated. Blue dye dropped to the bottom of the vats. Clear water rose to the top. The water was drained off. The dye was patted into cakes and put in the sun to dry. The cakes looked like blue mud pies.

By 1744, Eliza had 17 pounds of indigo to show for all her work. Of this, she sent six pounds to England. She hoped the clothmakers would try her dye.

Good news soon came from England. A letter was printed in the *South Carolina Gazette* in December of 1744. An Englishman wrote, "The Sample of Indigo sent here . . . has been tried and found better than the French Indigo."

Eliza wanted to share her success. Most of the 1744 crop was saved for seed. She gave many of these seeds to her neighbors. Soon, other planters were growing crops of indigo.

Because of Eliza, indigo became a major crop in South Carolina. By 1747, over 100,000 pounds were sold to England. In time, the colony sold a million pounds of dye to England every year.

The new crop helped everyone but the French. The South Carolina planters made money. Shipowners had another product to carry. English clothmakers now bought a very fine grade of dye at fair prices.

Eliza did not spend all her time working. She visited friends on nearby plantations. She went to weddings and funerals. She spent her Sundays at church in Charles Town.

After church the country people had
a chance to visit and trade news.

She wrote her brother, "Charles
Town . . . is a neat pretty place . . . .
the streets and houses regularly built;
the ladies and gentlemen gay in their
dress . . ., people of a religious turn of
mind."

Charles Town was an exciting city.
Ships from all over the world crowded
the harbor. Fine homes lined the
streets. Stores and markets held all
kinds of goods. The Dock Street
Theater put on plays. There was a lot
to do in the South Carolina capital.

Every Halloween, the people of
Charles Town had parties on King
George's birthday. The ladies wore
dresses of silk and satin over large
hoops. The men wore square-cut
coats, velvet breeches, and buckled
shoes. Everyone turned out.

"The Gov. gave . . . a ball at night
for the ladies on the King's birthday at
which was a Crowded Audience of
gentlemen and ladies," she wrote her
father. "I danced a minuet with your
old acquaintance Capt. Brodrick . . . ."

Colonel Lucas was glad to hear this
news. He wanted his daughter to get
married. In colonial days, parents
often picked mates for their children.
He wrote Eliza about settling down.

He named two men he thought
would make good husbands.

Eliza answered her father honestly.
She did not like either of the men.
One she hardly knew. The other she
would not marry for all "the riches of
Peru and Chili."

". . . a single life is my only
Choice," she told her father. ". . . as
I am yet but Eighteen, (I) hope you
will put aside the thoughts of my
marrying yet these 2 or 3 years at
least."

Four years passed before Eliza
decided to marry. Then Eliza picked
her own husband. He was Colonel
Charles Pinckney, a lawyer and
plantation owner. Eliza's parents liked
her choice.

Eliza Lucas and Charles Pinckney
were married on May 27, 1744. They
lived at Belmont, the Pinckney
plantation. Pinckney also built his
wife a town house in Charles Town,
five miles away.

The next few years were busy ones for Eliza. She raised indigo at Belmont. She planted oak, magnolia, and other trees. She still looked after her father's plantations.

Eliza started to produce silk. Mulberry trees were planted. The mulberry leaves were fed to silkworms. The worms spun cocoons of silk. These cocoons were dried. Then Eliza and her slaves unwound the silk threads of the cocoons. The thread was used to make silk cloth. The cloth was used to make silk clothes.

Eliza and Charles became parents. They enjoyed watching their young children learn.

Eliza and Charles thought
education was very important. Both of
them had gone to school in London.
Now the Pinckneys wanted the same
for Charles, Harriott, and Thomas.
In April of 1753, the whole family
moved to England, where the
children were put in school.

Eliza enjoyed her return to
London. Over half a million people
now lived there. Eliza found many
things to do. Shoppers could buy
almost anything they wanted. There
was Mrs. Salmon's Wax-works. There
were cockfights in Birdcage Walk.
There was opera in the Haymarket
and concerts in Westminster Abbey.

Without plantation duties, the
Pinckneys were free to enjoy the city.
They went sight-seeing. They saw
Shakespeare's plays at the theater in
Drury Lane. They made many friends
and enjoyed having them over to dine.

The Pinckneys spent five years in England. During their stay, war broke out between England and France. Much of the fighting took place in the North American colonies. Charles Pinckney began to worry about the safety of his plantations.

Charles and Eliza decided to sail for home in the spring of 1758. They took little Harriott with them, and left Charles and Thomas in school. Eliza did not like leaving them behind, but there seemed to be no other way. Both parents wanted the boys to have an English education.

A month after they reached South Carolina, Charles Pinckney got sick.

For three weeks he suffered from the fever and then died. Eliza wrote Charles and Thomas the sad news.

"You have met with the greatest loss, my children . . .," she told the boys. "Your dear, dear father, the best and most valuable of parents, is no more!"

Now Eliza had to take care of her family and plantation alone. After five years in England, the plantation needed much work. Buildings were repaired. Slaves got new clothing. Lost tools were replaced. Crops were planted and harvested under Eliza's watchful care.

Without her husband, Eliza took
great comfort in her daughter. By
now Harriott was studying geography
and writing letters to her brothers.
Like her mother, she enjoyed music
and took weekly harpsichord lessons.

Eliza missed her sons, but Charles and Thomas could not come home. Because of the war with France, travel between England and the colonies was dangerous. The boys stayed with friends in England and kept on with their education. Eliza wrote them often.

"What I fear most for you is warmth of temper," she told her eldest child. "Learn, my dear Charles, To subdue the first emotions of Anger."

"Take care, my much beloved child, of your health," she wrote Thomas. "Be a good child; mind your learning."

In 1763, England won the war with France and the two nations signed a treaty. Like all wars, this one had cost a great deal of money. England was deeply in debt. The English lawmakers, called Parliament, decided to raise money from taxes. For the very first time, they voted to tax the colonists.

From 1764 on, Parliament passed a number of tax laws. Each time, the colonists protested. Each time, Parliament set aside the laws, then passed new ones. Many colonists became angry with Parliament for taxing them. Then they blamed King George for not siding with them.

Eliza's family got deeply involved in these protests. While in England,

Charles and Thomas stayed loyal to South Carolina. After finishing law studies, both men returned home.

The young men quickly became rebel leaders. Both spoke against the right of Parliament to tax the colonies. Both urged the colonists not to buy English goods. Both joined the

South Carolina militia. Throughout the colonies, men like Charles and Thomas began to prepare for war.

In the spring of 1775, fighting broke out in Massachusetts. Eliza read all about it in the *South Carolina Gazette*. On April 19, English and American soldiers traded gunfire at Lexington and Concord. The war for independence had begun.

Many people were frightened by this news. The Pinckney brothers and other rebel leaders got ready to defend Charles Town. They built forts on islands in the harbor. They put cannon along the waterfront. There were always lookouts on duty.

It took a year for the war to reach South Carolina. In June of 1776, a fleet of English warships attacked Charles Town. The Americans were ready. The English fleet was badly hurt and sailed away.

The English tried a new plan. They captured Savannah, Georgia. The idea was to move north and take Charles Town by land. In the spring of 1779, a large force of English soldiers began marching towards the South Carolina capital.

By May, the troops reached Thomas Pinckney's plantation, Ashepoo. Eliza thought this home would never be in danger. She had taken all she had of value there. It was bad luck. The enemy was happy to raid a rebel's plantation.

"They took with them all the best Horses they could find, burnt the dwelling House and books, destroyed

all the furniture, china, etc., killed
the sheep and poultry and drank the
liquors," Thomas reported to Eliza.

Eliza's troubles were just beginning.
Both her sons were in great danger.
The English surrounded Charles
Town. In May of 1780, American
soldiers inside the city finally
surrendered. Colonel Charles
Pinckney was taken prisoner.

A few months later, Americans
fighting under General Gates were
beaten at the Battle of Camden. In
that battle, Major Tom Pinckney's leg
was badly hurt by a musket ball. For
weeks, Eliza's younger son was in
danger of losing his life.

All during this time, Eliza was staying with her daughter at Hampton plantation. They, too, were in danger. Once they were nearly caught as spies.

After fighting the English at Georgetown, Colonel Francis Marion, the famous Swamp Fox, rode into Hampton. He needed rest and food before going on. Harriott and Eliza fixed a hot meal as the weary rebel slept. Then the pounding of horses

was heard. The English were hot on
Colonel Marion's trail.

Out the back door went the Swamp
Fox. In the front door came the
English. They searched the house, but
not the grounds. An officer ate the
meal fixed for Colonel Marion, and
helped himself to a book from the
library. Then the English rode off.

With Eliza's help, the Swamp Fox had outfoxed the enemy once again.

In 1781 most of the fighting ended. The English lost at Yorktown. On December 14, 1782, the English flag came down in Charles Town. The King's troops sailed away. The Americans came into town as the enemy left. At last the state of South Carolina was free of English rule. The 13 colonies were now the 13 states of the United States. The Americans had won independence.

Eliza rejoiced to see the war end. But the Revolution had brought terrible hardships to her family.

"Both my Sons, their wives and Infants were exiled. . .," she wrote a friend in London. (My estate) "was shattered and ruined . . . . nor had I in Country or Town a place to lay my head . . . . all was taken from me, nor was I able to hire a lodging." She was glad it was over.

The last years of Eliza's life were filled with happiness. She spent much time with her daughter, Harriott, and her grandchildren. She saw her older son Charles join the new government under President Washington. Thomas became the governor of South Carolina.

"I now see my children grown up,
and blessed be God! see them such as
I hoped," she told a friend.

In 1791, Eliza met President
Washington. While touring the South,
he came to Harriott's plantation for
breakfast. Eliza and many of her
neighbors were there. They all
wanted to greet the new nation's first
President.

President Washington and Eliza
talked about the war. She praised his
faith in independence. He praised her

and her family's bravery during the war.

Eliza Lucas had been a hard-working young woman. She ran her father's plantations. She brought indigo to her colony. She helped other planters grow rich by sharing her indigo seeds with them.

Eliza Lucas Pinckney had been a strong wife. She married a man of her own choice. She bore and raised three fine children. Without a husband, she did the work of two parents.

Eliza Pinckney had been a brave rebel. She supported independence. During the Revolution she faced danger many times. She and her daughter aided rebel soldiers. Both her sons fought for the United States. One was wounded, one was captured.

The life of Eliza Pinckney shows us what southern ladies were really like. Eliza Pinckney brought about changes with hard work and new ideas. She was a woman of courage, strength, and purpose.

About the Authors:

Susan Dye Lee has been writing professionally since she graduated from college in 1961. Working with the Social Studies Curriculum Center at Northwestern University, she has created course materials in American studies. Ms. Lee has also co-authored a text on Latin America and Canada, written case studies in legal history for the Law in American Society Project, and developed a teacher's guide for tapes that explore women's role in America's past. The writer credits her students for many of her ideas. Currently, she is doing research for her history dissertation on the Women's Christian Temperance Union for Northwestern University. In her free moments, Susan Lee enjoys traveling, playing the piano, and welcoming friends to "Highland Cove," the summer cottage she and her husband, John, share.

John R. Lee enjoys a prolific career as a writer, teacher, and outdoorsman. After receiving his doctorate in social studies at Stanford, Dr. Lee came to Northwestern University's School of Education, where he advises student teachers and directs graduates in training. A versatile writer, Dr. Lee has co-authored the Scott-Foresman social studies textbooks for primary-age children. In addition, he has worked on the production of 50 films and over 100 filmstrips. His biographical film on Helen Keller received a 1970 Venice Film Festival award. His college text, *Teaching Social Studies in the Elementary School*, has recently been published. Besides pro-football, Dr. Lee's passion is his Wisconsin cottage, where he likes to shingle leaky roofs, split wood, and go sailing.

About the Artist:

Andy Aldridge was born in Alexandria, Virginia. His high school years were spent in Pasadena, California. He then attended the Art Center in Los Angeles. He worked in advertising and publishing illustration in New York and California, and has made his home in Chicago for the last 23 years. Andy has a lifetime interest in tennis and baseball and is currently coaching an intercity baseball team of teenagers.